I am, therefore I belong

Maliha Maisha Rahman

This one is for you, Ammu
For teaching me to be strong.
This one is for you, Abbu
For teaching me to be persistent
And for you, Tarik
For teaching me to love.

SANITY

Sanity

We have left the distance at a certainty,
So profane are the signs,
Cornered in obscurity–
Lured, tempted, trembled by us.

Perfection lies beneath imperfection.
Nothing that exists is mine,
Nothing that exists is yours;
We are in fact older than antiquity.
What that may ever be but
We still are.
And we belong.

Taken

It's written, printed and filmed
By those second man;
I woke up in their dream,
In their terminable thought,
And in their intricate expression.

I am, therefore I belong

It's signed, plated and carried
By the third man;
I lived in their hope,
In their traceable opinion,
And their illumined version.

It's geared, framed and shown
By the fourth man;
I am the time on their watch;
It goes on ticking slowly,
And they reveal themselves-
As my creators,
For here I seek a dead space,
As their watches have expired.

I am Del Esccanis

Together they rule.
One being alone, the other unworthy;
Their greater silence,
In a separation of latitude and time–
Revealed:
"Whatever must be announced, written and
kept, must be for pleasure"
Destroy those who have failed to speak!
Fixation occurring through scotoma...
Define it or be defined!

Maliha Maisha Rahman

The mind of a painter

She leaves through the door of darkness,
Complaining that the world is like a sponge,
Erasing the darkness
And soaking up the light.
"Isn't that alright?" they would ask.
"What would a blistered pig know about
being holy?" she thought,
But never answered.

I am, therefore I belong

She painted the path
with no house,
Painted the nude man
with no stroking muscle,
Painted the girl
with no urgency of sanity...
They never understood her mind
they hated her, spurned her–
"What would the one-legged dog know
about peace?" she thought
but never answered.

Her deep eyes x-rayed through the strangers'
eyes,
and she found only void.
Living there was just enough for them.

They were never there to be transformed,
she was never there to reveal–
It was the constancy of a motion,
she could never accept.
It was a different language she spoke,
Distant chamber she lived in,
Where only being there was not enough.

Agony

Here I am,
Left with a few submissive drops,
Agonized by the intrusion of a stranger.
As obscure as I am,
And as divine as my voice has appeared,
I say:
Let me be.
Let alone me be.

Time

A mystery comes,
comes to your wharf,
making all your love buried.
It stops you, a love-adept.
Slaves to not your lure
And never keeps a drop of tear to endure.

It floats in your boat,
Yet sails with supreme dominion,
Drinking all your fragrance
And breaking soul's ample-pinion.

It lines–
Lines an eternity,
And you, when the mystery leaves,
Become a yesterday

I am, therefore I belong

SOLITUDE

Soliloquy in the twilight

Vision of a light among the clouds,
that came striding,
As in a falling day.
She must think:
"Light comes from an ultimate end."

I am, therefore I belong

Repeating her thoughts,
She gathers and loses herself -where
Ascending and descending are the same.
Words, her border of thoughts,
So uncertain and profane,
Have spurned the beauty.
Which is too constant, the beauty that burns,
and too rare, the beauty that heals.

Losing demanding images,
She lures the uncertain age,
Something she never thought of.

I am, therefore I belong

Obscurity of her thoughts,
Is her concealed imagination,
for she made the imagination–
her god.

Lost

A January night,
Surrounded by a city crowd,
Speaking an obscure language.

The fog is deep and the cold is intense!
Vision is languid by a veil.
Walk!
Walk a long walk!
Lifeless naked lone trees,
Speaking an obscure language.

I am, therefore I belong

Wash the city off,
Diverge in the woods.
A forlorn sojourner,
frozen on a February morning.

Solitude

You stand out of your walls,
Seeing a restless earth moving beside you,
or the wind circling with the dust.
But you stand there at rest.

I am, therefore I belong

Everyone runs,
But you wait for the storm to come,
Seeing the grass grow together,
Soft and bending.
You perched on the grass
As the storm begins;
You wait for the mercy to come,
But it does not.

Maliha Maisha Rahman

The time goes on as it pleases,
You feel the cold, feel the wind,
Trying to tear you from your root,
But you hold on strong,
Trying to find yourself,
and avoid destruction.

I am, therefore I belong

The time goes on as it pleases,
And you find yourself at the end,
and no one to blame.
Because it is you,
who led a life of solitude.

Creation of September

Windows are framed by the silent
September,
Where the dry leaves await the wetness
of tomorrow's dew.

She stepped on the soaked sand,
A sightless touch of cold,
So wanted, so unborn.
Progressing on the stairs fails
leaving on each step a memory,
in obscure silence.

A seventh sense being theoremed:
"Who knew the urgency of creation?"
The profanity of having a wintered mind,
where acceptance of certainty
seemed impossible?
Crimson blood clotting in a straight line,
Who cut the hand–
She or the sharp edge of her knife?
Where was the true pain–
In the creation of the scar,
Or in being created?

I am, therefore I belong

LOVE

A moment of love

It was too easy,
Yet too sophisticated,
To be in love.
An emptiness was in their back,
Torturing them,
Ruling them,
Luring them.

I am, therefore I belong

It was closed,
Closed like a book,
Where the pages begged to get ink,
But words were forgotten,
And yet elegant,
If antiques on the cover got dusty,
To be remembered.

He liked the elegance of her,
she loved the white pages.
Too hard, yet too confident,
and a silence hovered over them both.

It was easy to live,
But it was hard to just be.

One night with a silent man

In an enchanting night,
A constant cry is made–
Silence it is.
She beholds in her hidden pain,
And that's what it is,
That mingled her with this night.

Words she had-
Were what she heard
That he tuned in silence.
And for an audience
Who would hear,
With a winter in the mind
Must fall in final.

The ultimate obscurity of his presence,
Is what his silence is,
For she made the silence–
Her god!

A prophecy of welcoming a soul,
That lives within her,
A lust of being a lust in him,
And a pale carnage beneath her
Leads to insanity.

No one, but within herself,
Who lives!
No one, she could lose the lust for,
No one that is!
But she believed herself–
That he exists.

Another night with a silent man

A breath on her neck,
Tuned the lyre beneath,
When she lost the lust for him.
With an uncertain fate,
Obscurity of his pensive tone,
Left her.
For that,
Fate was the only desire on the inside.

And the urgency of sanity,
Lived within the bare finger,
But it was dead;
As a consequence of a living diamond ring.

Nothing that is-
What was lost,
Except for her sign of finger,
On the edge of the smoky glass.
And nothing that is not,
What she wanted not to end.

The ultimate beauty lies in mind.
If that is,
They were above it.
A glimpse,
A gesture,
A sudden drop of tear,
believed to be-
The only creation of beauty.

Constant falling of snows,
Replace the old, sensual ones.
So virgin the unborn snows are,
That virgin she is!
For which the contentment of his carnage,
ends within her.

They lay there with their spent songs,
In an integration of the ultimate euphoria,
Where desire could exist no longer.
Dark folds of her skirt,
Conceal themselves,
Within the protruding edge of his shirt,
As if they lived beneath.

Maliha Maisha Rahman

Emblem of passion

Come from a dark depth
When water drops, tune the lyre–
And call it rain.

Come as my thoughts,
When I think about you–
And call it a dream.

Come as my voice,
When words create harmony–
And call it a song.

Come as my sorrow,
When a pearl arises from the sea–
And call it a tear.

Be my vision,
When a thousand colors dance together–
And call it a rainbow.

Be my shelter,
When I live within you–
And call it a home.

Be with me,
When I hide you behind everyone–
And call it a shadow.

Let your hands touch me,
When the moonlight touches the Earth–
And call it heaven.

Let your soul meet me,
When true souls give birth to a story–
And call it history.

I am, therefore I belong

Born as a sire of streams
and flow within my heart–
I will call it love.

Emblem of passion – memories

Silent memories spoke to me,
At the death of the day,
They came to me,
As a dream,
A dark, vintage dream.

They came to me,
When he had gone away with the wind,
Gone away,
In the deep silent land;
When his days drooped
And his foot no more stepped.

They came to me,
When his favorite book,
Was beneath the dust;
When his guitar tuned itself,
And his empty chair rocked.

They came to me,
When I remembered his paintings,
And when they painted me with sorrow.

They came to me,
And I remembered him
When he was lost among the stars,
When the leaves had a melancholy tear.

I am, therefore I belong

They came to me,
When I remembered his airy shroud,
Envied it for hugging him so close,
So close till the last moment.

They came to me,
When I remembered his gravestone,
With his name there,
And it made my heart ache in jealousy.

I saw all my memories,
When it came to me,
And kept coming,
Until my last breath came,
Until I transcended from life to death.
They kept coming to me
Until I met him in silent secret.

Desire

Lust he's held for so long,
As in a cloudy day,
He has lost in smoke,
Where a layer of tissues protrudes
on her face.

He lied beneath her,
A breath she took,
As in a winter day;
He has put a summer drop
On her protruding lips,
Where they both exist.

I am, therefore I belong

EXISTENCE

Beauty

A vintage moment,
Within eyes, proportioned perfectly.
In an integration of tissues, yet unveiled;
Obscurity is its ultimacy,
Where constancy is a change.

Beauty of nothingness

I saw a blind man,
When he walked through an isle,
Towards a child's pale face,
In an early summer light.

He walked and walked,
Seeing only dark with his eyes,
As his tapestries faded.

For obscurity of his vision,
They spurned him, loathed him,
Because their vision of mind,
was blind itself.

He believed in ultimate nothingness,
But their achievement in dark silence
Was unimagined.

I am, therefore I belong

They hold onto their antique portraits,
The paints grow subtle,
As their silence of solitude grows stronger.
His vision will only be granted
When they will believe
In the beauty of nothingness.

It's 3:00 a.m.

Constant dark fell upon the windows,
Until the light of moon,
Affixed its beam
On a dead night, I will be a life,
As my vision is reflected in the still fluid,
Concealed imagination revealed–
Endure enough to fall,
Until physiognomy alone is dead
leaving the face itself.

I am, therefore I belong

Loose enough to tune,
For an accordion has parted the diptych,
Or portray an image beneath
And reveal yourself as an allegory
For I would say you have lived enough!

Maliha Maisha Rahman

The wine and those eyes

In December it rained.
The wine glass stood still,
Deceived by those crystal raindrops;
The wine became those drops,
those drops became wine.

Those eyes were still-
wide open,
Deceived by those raindrops;
The urgency died,
The wine and those eyes were one,
Death lies dead.

Maliha Maisha Rahman

I saw a little boy sleeping on the footpath

I saw a little boy sleeping on the footpath;
He had a dream to see,
And a life to lead.

He slept in peace,
With a touch of a heavenly smile
With no thoughts or worries;
His face was innocent
and the body was naked
Had no fear of losing
For he had nothing to lose.

What dream he has–
a red shirt and a good amount of food?
What peace he has–
of no worries and woes or of his little
wants?
What pain he has–
of the life, to be lived or to die?

Maliha Maisha Rahman

The little boy has a life on the footpath,
under those stars,
And our lives are trapped in this human
snare-
lurking, demanding, dreaming, aiming for an
unknown peace and pain.

I saw an old smiling

I saw an old man smiling,
When he had a life to live
And a death to die.
The wayward smile followed the sun,
When the pale face was shrouded in
sunlight.
And his face shone like a mirror,
And I saw the morn' light curve near his face
When dawn died in there.

He smiled at me,
And I found his lost youth there,
When he possessed the world,
and his days,
When he tuned his flute,
And the woes of all village wives were
whispered away,
Away with soft dying notes.

The smile was not fraught with
ignorance of pain,
Nor was it wreathed with paint,
But covered with a veil of pain,
Made of happy memories.
I didn't find a drop of tear
Neither hate nor pride or fear,
All I found,
Was joy.

In the downhill of his life's page,
He didn't remember the death of his wife
Nor the death of his son,
He had nothing to lament,
All he had was hope and desire.

He smiled at me;
His mute silence had his voice and his
words,
And it made me smile;
The joy, the peace, the hope this smile gives,
Humans all over the world should choose to
live.

I saw a lady with a pale face

I saw a lady with a pale face,
When her life was sketched-
only to satisfy needs;
Those feelings were never heard-
Before they were felt;
Pain was never burnt
Before it attacked the breath of life.

77

I am, therefore I belong

'

Civilization spurns her,
For she is earth's third child,
Not deceiving or deprived.

Civilization is what drama is,
A lie, a curse!
Mournful–all its deeds of carnage,
were wafted with yesterdays,
for humanity would be defeated today.

A pantomime, her life be,
When sterner desires we keep to be,
Bathyllus!
If not stern, but blind for sure!

We call ourselves civilized!
Oh! civilization,
a meager sanity,
hardly humanity!

Maliha Maisha Rahman

To the sky

She held the fear of the rain,
Held the passion of heaven,
Dazzling light of the sun,
And the soft dim light of the moon.

She was weary and worn;
Her pale face-
expressed deep agony,
Told the truth unspoken-
She has no limit of her boundary
But has no existence.
She starts from a void
And ends in there

Maliha Maisha Rahman

A soldier's letter to his mother

Bugles sang truce,
For the pitch-dark of the night.
I lied on my bed and tried to sleep
Though I was tired enough.

I had a dream:
An antique face burning on a blazing pyre,
A body covered with a shroud;
I screamed and woke up.
In the dark,
In its silence,
My thoughts wandered away,
From this battlefield's dreadful array.

I am, therefore I belong

My thoughts took me to you, Mother,
To your smiling face,
And our sweet memories.
I remembered your words,
And I remembered you;
There is little time left for this bare winter,
To become spring.
But I am scared,
I am scared of this dark,
And of this world colored crimson in blood.
Will this world be my last place to live?
Will I fail to give all these letters to you,
Mother?
Will I be killed by these demons?
Will I fail to save our country,
From their evil grasp?

I am afraid, Mother,
Afraid of this world.
Suppress my fear with your love, Mother,
Give me strength,
And make me brave.

Bugles sang again,
A new sun arose,
And a new leaf was born.
Give me your love,
And let me reborn,
For then,
I will conquer all.

Story of a pornai

She had a veil,
But her dark red lips were showing;
She had a dress,
But her body curves were showing;
She had a wild look,
That captured his heart.

As he observed her closely,
she rose her veil–
God himself had taken care of her beauty,
and he became the slave to it.

She had a body language,
That was a lure to him;
It killed him with soft notes,
And as the chords tuned,
the world became a rainbow.

"You have money," she asked.
This was the first time he saw her lips
moving,
Her words baffled him.
"Why are you so surprised? I am a pornai
after all," she said.
He was stunned;
He wanted a girl, not a mindless body.
With no words, he shoved some notes in her
hand,
Notes they call money,
and strode away.

I am, therefore I belong

She gazed after him and thought:
I am a prostitute,
And this is a commercial world.
I earn food with my beauty
does that make me a commodity?
She wanted her beauty to be loved,
not to be sold.
She did not want to be under a vintage roof,
she only wanted to be a girl under a blue,
sunny sky.
She sighed,
And left her dreams under their civilized
sky.

Maliha Maisha Rahman

If I were a poem...

If I were a poem,
A thought filled with perennial dreams,
A vision filled with rainbows,
Words made of vintage letters,
And a voice full of songs.

If I were a poem,
Floating like the clouds,
Dancing in the rain,
Like sunshine on the streams.

I would become a poem,
If thoughts had a melancholy cry,
And letters were born by those drops of tear,
When memories had silent nights with a
shut heart.
Words had a pain of those memories,
When rhythm had a crimson mistake,
And pages went red by those rhythms.

Now, I am a poem.
A poem with drooping words,
A poem with a recluse rhythm,
A poem of hidden pain,
kept untouched.

Here I am,
A poem of scattered words,
To be lost in old weary pages.

The poet

How your words are written,
Being a harmony,
With a boundless symphony,
One after another–beautiful!

I am, therefore I belong

How your feelings flow,
Being exposed,
Being a secret,
Being a beauty against the twilight!

How your silence works,
Absorbing me,
Taking me to the grandeur age,
Where I seek happiness.

Oh, poet!
Take me, lure me,
Make me a slave of your silence,
For a journey to an unknown sphere;
A slave of your imagination,
That brings spring in my timeless moments.

Last letter

I wrote my last letter,
Giving dreams a shroud,
Surrendering to the mistakes,
And intensifying my agony.

I wrote the last letter,
In the dark cavern of the page,
Trying hard not to cross the line;
But my ebony words walked over the line
and the death came as destruction.

I am, therefore I belong

ABOUT THE AUTHOR

Maliha Maisha Rahman is a young-adult contemporary poet. At an early age, she had found love for poetry and her poems portraits sign of hardships and all the human ailments and needs.

Maliha Maisha Rahman was born and raised in Bangladesh. She came to the USA at the age of 24 to pursue masters in mechanical engineering. She is now 27, living in Michigan with her husband.

On her blog, she talks about her journey from Bangladesh to the USA and the path to success that she had opened for herself. If you want to know more about her life, journey and literature, visit her website: www.life-as-an-international.com